Proclaiming Your Divine Birthright:

Affirmations

Other books by this author

Archangel's, Ascended Master's, God's Goddesses and Affirmations
©Khadija Franklin 2019

Archangels, Ascended Masters and Divinities: Guide to Working with Divinities
New Edition ©Khadija Franklin 2020

Proclaiming Your Divine Birthright:

Affirmations

KHADIJA FRANKLIN

ISBN: 978-1-8382681-2-1
Independently Published

Cover and Logo Design: Raymond Wade

How Can Affirmations Change Your Life?

If you are reading this book; you have decided to take the necessary action to change your life. As Divine Beings, we are here on a soul evolutionary journey. transforming continuously from limited human consciousness to limitless Divine, spiritual consciousness.

Affirmations are positive statements that help us overcome negative thoughts and self-sabotaging false beliefs.

As humans, we have been programmed with historical dramas, false perception, and suffering. Many people don't even realise that the words they speak can be self-sabotaging and self-harming. Words have the power to influence you both negatively and positively daily. Words have different vibrational frequency and create your reality.

It's fundamental to pay attention to your thoughts and the words you speak.

Do you notice that when you start your day saying positive affirmations, your day becomes a magnet for positive people and circumstances to assist you? Whatever you believe, the Universe says, "your wish is my command." It gives you what you ask for—which is influenced by your predominant thoughts.

Hence, the Universe will rearrange itself and bring the right people and circumstances to fulfil your beliefs.

View affirmations as if they are physical exercises. If you want to keep in shape, you exercise every day for some time, or you make it your lifestyle and every day you see an improvement in your appearance.

It's the same for your mind; you need to exercise and train your mind to think differently. Negative thoughts can become self-fulfilling prophecies, and the result can affect your personal lives, your relationships, and your careers. Hence, positive affirmations mitigate stress, anxiety, worry, and boost your happiness and energy. You feel motivated and confident; you also find people are attracted to you because of the positive energy you exude.

When you use positive thoughts, you are clearing the negative programming that was subconsciously embedded in you without you even realising it.

Regardless of your belief system, affirmations have one purpose: to make life better. No matter how pessimistic your thoughts have become, you can reprogram your subconscious mind and begin to think differently.

When you repeat a phrase or line to yourself over and over again, your mind eventually starts to believe it. The more your mind believes, the greater chance you have to manifest your hopes and dreams into reality.

This is the almighty power of the mind when combined with the eternal power of the universe—the ability to manifest the life you need to live—one of health and happiness.

Below is a list of affirmations that I have found personally helpful and transformative for me, and I would like to share them with you, so that you, too, may benefit from the incredible power of affirmations.

They are divided into groups: one for believers in God and the Universe, and one for people who feel more comfortable believing not in a powerful entity, but themselves.

I recommend doing the affirmations in the morning before you start your day. However, you should do what feels right for you. Affirmations can be truly life changing. The positive vibration you send out into the universe, will attract the same vibration back to you. By implementing them daily, you slowly change your thinking, and things begin to happen that you never thought possible.

If you devote yourself to the affirmations daily, you will begin to experience the magic of positive thinking. You will become happier, have more energy, and be motivated to follow your dreams and bring them to fruition. You will sail through life with ease and exude tremendous love in your heart.

Table of Contents

How Can Affirmations Change Your Life? v

My personal journey with affirmations. xi

PART ONE

Powerful Affirmations: Asked and it's Forgiven 14

PART TWO

Powerful Transforming Self-Affirmations 30

PART THREE

Self-Gratitude Affirmations Directed to God 119

Gratitude to God and our Guides ... 119

Family Gratitude Affirmations 132

Mother Earth Gratitude Affirmations 137

PART FOUR

How Affirmations Can Change Your Life 142

My personal journey with affirmations

Before I discovered affirmations and comprehended the benefits of using them, I would ask for what I don't want. For example, the more I affirmed, "I don't want *this*", "I don't want *that*", the more the universe mirrored what I don't want back to me because the universe doesn't know that I *didn't* want it. It only knows that these are my strong feelings, so that's what I got, so I don't think I am crazy.

Affirmations have helped me in my journey and during my difficult times. They have shown me how I can easily change the vibration around me by affirming positive words to myself.

Growing up in a dysfunctional family constantly being told I wasn't good enough and would amount to nothing, really destroyed my self-esteem and feeling of self-worth.

I used to be my own worst critic, and I would criticise myself for every little mistake I made; even for other peoples' actions toward me because I have been programmed to believe the worst about myself. Also, I was a people pleaser because I didn't value myself.

Not until I started using affirmations was I able to shift my projective beliefs. It wasn't easy at first, but I knew that every time I used affirmations, I felt happier, motivated, and I could feel my heart glowing with love. My soul was smiling every time I said positive words to myself.

I was determined as I persisted to rid myself of my negative programming. You see, my parents—and other peoples'—beliefs of me don't define who I am. My own beliefs are what defines me. I was born perfect, and I am perfect, so I make my own beliefs that are true for me.

I am not the same person I was years ago on any level physically, energetically, emotionally, or spiritually.

When I started, I struggled, and it was uncomfortable saying positive words to myself. I kept falling back into the rabbit hole over and over again.

With any new habit, it takes determination and resilience. Once I started to change within myself, my outer surroundings began to change. As a result, I was attracting the right people and circumstances into my energy field.

I was surprised the first time I looked in the mirror and said: "I love you." I couldn't do it. It took a month for me to look myself in the eye and say, "I love you", without my ego telling me I was lying and feeling uncomfortable about it. Now I have no problem looking into my eyes, telling myself how much I love and appreciate myself, smiling at myself and making funny faces. I enjoy doing it now. Whenever I feel sad, I go straight to the mirror.

I also don't fall consciously into victimhood as easily anymore, and I don't stay there as long. Instead, I can see and dismantle the drama I face and create and liberate my soul with the power of my spirit.

My transformation happened with continuous focus on changing my thinking and transforming my vocabulary into positive words about myself and my circumstances.

ONE

Powerful Affirmations

Asked and it's Forgiven

Thank You, God, for helping me face my controlling fears which contributed to the challenges in my life.

I meet my fears head-on, releasing them and healing them so I can fully enjoy my life experiences.

Thank you, God, for helping me to overcome any resistance to living my life. To embrace my Divinity, manifest my dreams, and live an authentic and fulfilled life.

God, I humbly ask to be a channel of love and light to my brothers and sisters on Earth, to shine bright wherever I go, and to open my heart fully.

God, bless me with your omnipresent grace to empower me to surrender my ego's control fully.

Enable me to move beyond my comfort zone and experience life's magnificent abundance.

God, I pray that you free me from my ego and people's untruths that keep me from living my full potential, enabling me to have a happy and authentic life.

God, I asked that you free me from lies, shame, guilt, anger, and release me from painful, difficult life experiences I've heard.

Please bestow your all-empowering grace upon me—now and forever.

God, surround me with your Benevolent Heavenly Beings, to give me the courage to step in the direction of my heart's desire, and to be a loving example to my brothers and sisters.

God, keep me mindful of my actual place in the universe and to remain conscious and loving always when dealing with myself and others.

Guide my heart to be honest with myself and others, and to remain Faithful.

God, give me the confidence and courage to follow my heart's desire. To remember my divinity, and to be a co-creator in my life journey.

Thank you, God, for my creativity and my skills to succeed in life.

My imagination reflects my authentic spirit. I recognize and celebrate my beautiful gifts.

Thank you, God, for always answering my prayers; for guiding and providing for all my needs. And for the never-ending fantastic opportunities and people, you send my way.

Thank you, God, for reminding me to be aware of all the love and abundance that is coming to me every day and for my incredible, fulfilling life experiences.

I have nothing to fear for I am protected by God. I am free and capable to create magnificent projects and opportunities to share with my human brothers and sisters.

Thank you, God, for my ability to express my authentic self. For the love and laughter that I give and receive, with all my interactions, and for my witty sense of humour.

Thank you, God, for my grateful, loving heart. I share the love with everyone I come in contact with, and every person I touch, and who touches me, is a healing exchange.

Thank you, God, for the abundance of love that is available to me and for my open heart and mind which knows no limit.

I bask in the knowledge that I am never separated from God. I am for ever more connected to God. All I have to do is open my heart and feel God's love.

I receive inspiration and guidance from God. All my inspiration comes from unconditional love.

I am blessed with the fortitude to walk through all my losses and difficulties with unwavering faith and dignity. God and the Angels are my constant companions on This Earthly plane.

I am empowered with endless possibilities. I accept that I am God's magnificent, brilliant child, and I am experiencing all the good the universe has to offer me.

Whenever I am worried about negative emotions, God and the Angels clear my mind and guide me toward making the right decision.

God and the Angels watch over me. I am always safe and bathed in God's love.

I am happy and grateful for my journey so far. I trust God to continue guiding and providing for me. I trust in divine timing.

God is supporting me in everything I do. I am a great healer, and I love healing others and myself. I am grateful for my gifts. God and the Angels value me and love me unconditionally. I am loved just for being myself.

I communicate clearly with God and my Guides. I truly express myself, and I listen deeply and pay attention to their guidance. I asked God and the Angels to assist me with everything in my life. I am eternally connected to heaven.

When I am feeling low and sad, I ask God to surround me with love and more angels to lift my spirit. I am surrounded by Divine love.

I release all my worries and illusions to God. God shines a light in all my situations, filling my body, mind, and heart with Divine love. I am God's precious child, and I am loved unconditionally.

I stop limiting myself and surrender to God and the universe. I release my worries, fears and manifest my desires. Whenever I am in doubt, I surrender my worries and welcome Divine intervention. I was born to be prosperous. I am a blessing to this world. God shines light in all my situations, and I am filled with divine, healing light.

I thank God in advance for hearing my prayers and for showering my life with endless gifts, opportunities and for my colourful, prosperous life.

I have nothing to fear. God is always with me, guiding and protecting me. My creator loves me unconditionally.

I stop limiting myself and surrender to God. I release my worries, fears and manifest my desires. I was born to be prosperous. I am a blessing to this world. God shines light in all my situations, and I am filled with divine, healing light.

Thank You for hearing my prayers and for showering my life with endless gifts, opportunities and for my colourful, prosperous life.

God and the Angels remind me of my greatness every time I am tempted to judge myself harshly or condemn myself. I become centred, calm and surrounded in Divine loving, healing light.

I eliminate and remove all uncooperative willingness and surrender to God and my spirit. I follow through with what I came here to do and accomplish all my divine plans.

Whenever I feel empty, unworthy and overwhelmed, I ask God and the Angels to grace and lift my spirit. I feel all the goodness and love that surrounds me. I am loved, and I love unconditionally.

Every time I feel vulnerable, God, help me have compassion and love for myself and to hold kind accepting thoughts towards myself and to know that I am doing the best I can.

Thank you, God, for bestowing your All-Empowering Grace upon me. I live in truth with my spirit. I speak with clarity and purpose, and with a depth of understanding in every conversation.

I am happy and grateful for my journey so far. I trust God to continue guiding and providing for me. I trust in divine timing.

When I am feeling low and sad, I ask God to surround me with love and more angels to lift my spirit. I am surrounded by Divine love.

TWO

Powerful Transforming Self-Affirmations

My heart is filled with deep gratitude for everything that has been made available to me, and for this beautiful planet where I have my life experiences.

My soul is evolving rapidly with every life experience.

I choose to engage in conversations that are uplifting and inspiring. I choose the materials I read and the entertainment I enjoy.

I free my mind from the fear of the unknown and not having enough. I focus on everything I need, which is provided for me, and every day is an excellent, fulfilling adventure.

I override my ego and overcome my fears; I focus on transforming my life and achieving everything that my heart desires, for 1 manifest instantaneously.

Anything that is not good for me, I eliminate immediately. I am strong, authentic, and capable, and I focus on what fulfils my life.

I allow myself to feel my emotions; however, my emotions don't control me. I am strong, powerful, capable, and all-knowing. I am a wise, loving warrior.

I share my incredible gifts with the world. I uplift and nurture my surroundings and my world. I spread love and knowledge wherever I go.

I am a shining light in this world, and I happily share this light with everyone I meet.

I demonstrate strong and authentic leadership. I indulge in positive and fulfilling subjects that help the Whole.

I eliminate procrastination and fearlessly dive into my creative projects. I happily share my creation with the world.

My incredible mind loves to create beautiful, uplifting projects which help support others in their life journey.

I am gifted with the ability to share knowledge and help heal the world. I am a naturally gifted healer.

I am empowering, nurturing, and inspirational. My personality is lovingly magnetic.

I take full responsibility for everything I do, and I make everything better and excellent.

I allow myself to dwell only on positivity. I easily control my emotions. I am calm, strong, capable, and loving. I know what to do, and I do everything right.

All my dealings with others are loving and refreshing. I love learning from the people around me and my surroundings.

I am a brilliant thinker and fast, vigorous learner. I love sharing my incredible healing work with the world.

I love connecting, observing people, and learning incredible things. I also love connecting within and sharing my insights.

I appreciate everything that has been given to me, and like a child, I eagerly await every day for new experiences, which are loving and inspiring.

I follow through with my commitments. I am centered and unwavering with everything I put my focus on.

I am blessed with never-ending supplies. All the people I meet are wise and helpful teachers who add to my life in miraculous ways.

As brothers and sisters, we work together to make this world a better place for everyone.

I speak kindly and calmly. I have established self-respecting boundaries for myself, and I uphold these standards; I rise above offensive behaviours. Every day, I move through serenity and peace.

I am patient with myself and others. I banish all weakness, lies and inadequacies from my life completely. I live fully in the moment with integrity and wholeness.

I release all feelings of being stuck and scattered in the past. I focus on healing and raising my vibration to a level that served me and the whole. I am unlimited and capable of miraculous wonders.

I listen carefully to others when they speak to me, opening my heart and mindfully understand their conversation so that I can hear their point of view.

I refuse to entertain negative or condemning thoughts about myself, I release all self-sabotaging thoughts to heaven and focus on knowing how wonderful, capable, and beautiful I am inside out.

I easily detach from negative situations and negative people. I entertain and accept positive situations and positive people in my life.

I free myself from all addictions or unconscious behaviours that no longer serve me or my purpose. I focus my willpower on the things that service my life and add to other people's lives.

Instead of getting angry or worked up when I encounter difficult and stressful situations, I remember my power and strength. I bring a healing and positive attitude to the situation. I focus on love and all the happiness I have that surrounds me every day. I am capable of being, and it is easy for me to solve any problem.

I am patient and mindful of any situation I encounter. I don't let human mistakes bother me for we are all doing the best we can. However, I have the right to remove myself from any situation that no longer serves me.

Every time my ego is chattering fearful or unpleasant shutters in my mind, I tell it to take a nap and have a rest. I am in control of my ego because I am powerful and all-knowing.

Insecurities are a false imprint. My open-mindedness and willingness to learn is uncompromisable.

I am joyously working towards enlightenment.

I am surrounded with guidance, friendship, humour, laughter and abundance throughout my life. Everything is made easy for me, and I can accomplish everything I want with ease.

I know who I am, and I recognise my worth. I am confident, and I always speak my truth, no matter what. My honesty and truth cannot be compromised.

I accept everything that unfolds before me today. I accept pain, but I don't capitulate to pain. Pain is a reminder to examine my thoughts and surroundings.

Disappointment does not affect me or my life. Disappointment makes me wiser and more robust and help me to focus on what's essential in my life.

I welcome good and bad experiences in my life. I need to experience both circumstances in order to evolve in my life's journey. What matters is how I handle the experiences.

Every day I try my best to keep myself from succumbing to my fears. I stay centered, grounded, and strong as I tread on unfamiliar ground.

I am flexible and adaptable to all changes. I face my fears without resistance and rejection. I am courageous and dignified when faced with challenges. I focus on my greatness.

Whenever I experience the feeling of disappointment and frustration, I quickly look within and release the emotion from my mind and body, focusing instead on peace and serenity.

There is always growth, lessons to be learned and beneficial experiences that stem from disappointment. I am grateful and happy to have the ability to accept whatever unfolds before me with dignity.

I joyfully surrender everything that stresses me, which is not for my highest good. I do this easily, and I focus my energy on positivity in my life.

I let my light shine bright and destroy negativity with laughter and my all-empowering grace.

I laugh at myself and all my mistakes and take nothing that occurs too seriously. I let myself enjoy the silliness of life and its wonders.

I appreciate all my creativity and my abilities to see beauty, as well as to create beauty and wonders in my world.

I see every opportunity that lies before me and relish them with delight.

I don't sit still during my favourite music, enjoying every beat of my heart being free; in serenity, I dance my way to fulfilment.

I transmute all debilitating resentment into love and gratitude; I am whole, perfect, and capable.

My life, from the day I was born until the day I leave, is magical. In my eyes, I only see magic wonders and magnificent, exciting experiences.

I love to share; I am here to grow and learn and help. I am magnificent Divine Being discovering the magical adventure that is called Life.

I Am a light-hearted, easy-going, entertaining, joyful, and brilliant thinker with unlimited creative abilities.

I have the power to make people happy with my laughter. With my laughter and vibrant attitude, I clear all negativity in the atmosphere I am in; I remove tension and stress from the people around me.

I am blessed with muses from heaven. My mind is filled with creativity and new perspectives. I love entertaining myself and others with my creativity.

I am strong enough to stop negative conversation and grumbling when talking to people. I break free from negative patterns, habits and behaviours that no longer serve me.

My Divine Creator blessed me with pure happiness and the ability to spread healing and love wherever I go.

I face my wounds from the past and heal them completely.

I reconstruct my experiences with humour, objectivity and detachment. What defines me is what I choose to believe.

I am truly grateful for all the friends in my life and especially for those who have been there for me, through thick and thin. I am so thankful for their loving support and comforting companionship.

I celebrate all of my relationships. My relationships are surrounded by love. My friends are constantly supporting and adding to my life journey.

I am centred and mindful of my blessings. I receive, and I take nothing for granted; however, I enjoy the fullest of everything that is offered to me.

My mind is filled with loving thoughts towards myself, and I forgive all my mistakes. I appreciate my beautiful, unique self. I am thankful for my ability to banquet my blessings.

I genuinely love and have affection for myself. I am courageous, confident, authentic, and true to myself in every way.

I am gifted with abundant energy. I move with ease and fluidity every day. I am filled with exuberance and laughter every day and forever.

I have the ability and willpower during difficult times to nurture my spirit, meditate and connect within. I can feel the Presence of my Divine Creator surrounding me with love, healing, and comforting light.

I communicate with whomever I am conversing with freely and calmly. I express my feelings with strength, dignity, and love.

I inspire everyone I meet to speak their truth with authenticity and an open heart.

I am blessed with resilience through difficult times, and I am brilliant at shining my light and moving forward with full speed to achieve my dreams.

I am gifted with the ability to uplift and inspire even the most cynical and jealous person. I help them to see the truth and change their perspective and outlook on life, as well as to focus on self-healing and love.

I am always loving and generous to others, and I appreciate them for the difference they make in my life.

Acknowledging we are here to grow and support one another is important to us all.

I live my life fully, and I am adventurous. I am unique, unapologetic, loving and colourful. I am gifted with unlimited abilities to accomplish all my dreams.

I remove competitiveness from my life. I know that there is plenty for everyone, and I accomplish all my goals with love and ease.

I am attentive and caring towards myself, my family and friends, and whenever I am needed, I am there to give comfort and laughter.

I shape and reshape my reality whenever I choose. I am focused and determined; I am a winner in whatever I want. I achieve it with ease.

No matter what is going on around me or in my country, I can achieve my dreams if I want to. I am the creator of my destiny.

I am free and courageous. I continuously evolve myself and reach for the stars.

Every day I am overflowing with joy. Everything in my life is terrific, and I am beaming with confidence

I remove myself from negativity and disrespectful people.

I move forward with authenticity and an open heart; I know how special and consequential I am.

Fantastic opportunities surround me every day. I quickly transform into a beautiful, better me.

I face everything with strength and love. Every experience is filled with abundant creative possibilities and stimulates me.

All conditions I meet, I quickly transform into positivity and a brilliant opportunity to use my brilliant mind to achieve my will.

I was born in the perfect condition to help my soul grow. All my experiences gave my soul the perfect opportunity to evolve. I love to share my experience with my human brothers and sisters to help them on their journey.

I understand my childhood conditioning, and I take full advantage in learning from it. I am continuously developing and using all the lessons positively to empower myself and others.

I turn all negatives into positives, for I know only love and gratitude will open the gates of manifestation, which brings me the happiness and prosperity I deserve.

I am always conscious of choosing a better, healthier, and simple life for myself. I am mindful of my surroundings.

I turn all my circumstances into a productive outcome that serves me and help others. I am generous, and all of my qualities are lovely.

I gracefully meet all my needs without sacrificing what's important to me. I am gifted with the ability to do everything right.

I take full responsibility for my life, and I invest my energy and productivity into achieving my dreams.

I ignore judgement and focus on my qualities, knowing that I have a brilliant mind that is capable of achieving whatever I want.

I don't let emotions cloud my judgement. I refrain from being overly sensitive and reactive. For I know, I am strong, powerful, capable, and loving.

I am mature, and I accept challenges. I grow through my challenges, and I am determined to improve and grow.

When one relationship ends, better and loving relationships come into my life. It's okay for me to let go, and I am always surrounded by love.

I welcome advice, but ultimately, I listen to my advice. I am wise, and I have all the answers inside of me.

I take criticism, but criticism doesn't define me. For I know my worth and I am loved.

My parents' beliefs are their own. I follow my own beliefs from my own experiences and choose my path.

I respect others' beliefs, and I follow the beliefs that are right for me. I am wise, and I know what is suitable for me.

I don't rely on people to respect me, because the respect that matters the most is the respect that I have for myself.

I don't wait for anyone's approval because I take the right action for me. I always know what the best thing to do for me.

I compliment myself every day because I deserve it, and I welcome compliments with open arms.

I seek people who add meaning to my life and encourage me to reach for the stars.

I am a creative being, and I create every day, no matter how small. I have a profound creative mind that loves to create.

I love expanding my mind and learning something new every day. I am capable of everything I do, and I am brilliant.

I choose to focus my mind on wealth. Being wealthy is my natural birthright. I am wealthy.

I love looking good and looking in the mirror and saying, "I love you."

I have a loving and healthy relationship with myself.

We all act differently to situations, so I listen, observe and take in what is of service to me.

Money is exchanged energy. I love money, but I choose not to stress about it.

I pamper myself because I deserve it. I express joy and gratitude for all my abundance in my life.

I am honest with myself, and I am honest with others because the truth always sets me free.

I forgive myself for being hard on myself and judging myself. I am doing the best I can.

Whenever I am in doubt, I surrender my fears and welcome Divine intervention.

I honour my divinity, and it's okay to be assertive. I send love to me today and in my future.

I speak kindly to myself, and I think positive thoughts, for I am a perfect divine being in human form.

My mistakes help me to become greater. I am stronger than I give myself credit for. I acknowledge my strength and wisdom.

Intimacy is healthy and wonderful. I honour my sexuality, and I allow myself to experience deep connection.

It is okay to be expressive, and I happily express my emotions.

I have the necessary skills to demonstrate and masterfully accomplish everything that I desire. I have unlimited talent and capability to succeed in everything I want.

I am skilled and gifted beyond comprehension, and I distribute my gifts and talents to the world. My creations are empowering, uplifting. and loving.

I easily release blame and guilt from my life, and I take responsibility for my actions.

I talk to my angels and guides every day, and I engage them in every decision involving my life.

I am beautiful inside out, and I only notice the beauty in me and around me.

I attract wonderful and loving people into my life and all of my relationships are amazing.

I am filled with wonders and I am adventurous. My life experiences are thrilling and inspiring.

I breathe in love and exhale anything that no longer serves me.

I dream big and my imagination is limitless.

I am always responsible for my life and I gladly take charge of my life.

I am a Divine Being with unlimited potential and I appreciate life and seize every opportunity.

The Universe provides me with endless possibilities. I choose wisely and appreciate all that I receive.

I choose to focus on people's positive side and that is what I get more of all the time.

I acknowledge both good and bad experiences in my life and I see them both as an opportunity to learn and grow.

I am capable of achieving what I want, no matter what is going on around me. I choose each day to live my life fully and achieve my dreams.

I infuse laughter and joy into my life. The more joy I add to my life, the more happiness I experience. I am blessed with an amazing life.

I base decision on fact, honesty and integrity when dealing with situations because I am powerful and wise.

When my actions are positive and empowering, I empower others to follow suit.

I am powerful and confident. I trust my judgement and decisions.

I am free of hardship and suffering. I am proud of who I am, all that I have and will achieve.

My light brightens shadows. I am constantly surrounded by love and light. I cherish my brilliant mind that is continuously evolving.

I flow freely with life. Life is wonderful, exciting and an adventure.

Life is precious and I follow my dreams. I can do anything I put my mind to. I love what I do.

Everyone is entitled to their own opinion. Criticism is just that. My reaction ear is always confident, positive, and loving.

I am at peace, no matter what. I swim in the tranquility that surrounds me and flow with life.

My consciousness is filled with love and happiness and I mirror this with everyone I meet.

It easy for me to attract great things and wonderful people into my life.

Life supports me abundantly. I appreciate all that I have, and I am grateful.

As I open my heart and share my opportunities, the universe provides greater opportunities for me to share.

I accept my unique individuality and I approve of myself. I love myself.

Age is just a number, and my imagination and power are limitless. I am stronger, confident, wiser and I can achieve anything I want.

I am patient, I am in the right place at the right time. The universe will open the doors that are right for me.

All the cells in my body radiate love, health and joy. I make time to reflect upon what is important in my life, and I nurture my body.

I am an alchemist; I manifest my dreams and desires easily, because I have faith in my abilities.

I am receptive to new opportunities. I am happy and grateful as I embark on my daily adventure.

I always honour my words and the commitments I make to myself and others.

The more I love, respect, appreciate and accept myself, the more these will mirror me.

Everything happens for a reason and each change or experience brings positive opportunity.

I express my creativity by allowing my imagination and abilities to flow freely. My creativity is a true expression of who I am.

I have incredible family, great friends, and a harmonious life.

My imagination has no limitation. I am grateful, capable, blessed, and I embrace life's challenges as an opportunity to stretch myself.

I release my limiting beliefs and let my imagination run freely; I reach for the stars.

My body is my best friend and I trust my body's wisdom. I nourish, support, love and respect my body.

The more I am grateful, the more the universe provides for me. I focus on gratitude and love.

I enjoy making new friends and reinforcing exciting relationships. I respect them and we uplift each other.

Today I stop blaming others and take full responsibility for my life. I am a powerful creator, and I create my life experiences.

I express myself openly to my family and friends and we support each other.

How I feel inside is what I mirror to others, so I choose love with all its abundance.

Nothing external can diminish me. For I am worthy, powerful, content, happy and true to who I am.

I don't need others' approval to be happy. I am an amazing Divine Being with unlimited potential. I am proud of myself.

Whatever I imagine, I receive, so I choose to imagine what I want. The universe delivers everything that I ask for.

I release judgement from my life. I demonstrate love, honour and compassion.

Good and bad experiences give me the opportunity to examine the difference. I allow myself to experience both and choose the path of love and positivity.

Every day I live to the fullest. I am in school on Earth, learning with my brothers and sisters.

I acknowledge and respect other people's boundaries. All of my relationships are based on mutual respect, honesty and understanding.

I embrace all my flaws, and I love and accept myself exactly as I am.

I add value and make a positive difference to the world; I am a treasure to the world.

I do what I can every day to help Mother Earth and my environment.

I am excited and passionate about my goals and I focus on dreaming big.

Every day I make a difference where possible. No matter how small, I rejoice in doing my part.

Every experience is a lesson for me to learn and grow. I choose my words and thoughts carefully because they create my reality.

I receive with open heart and I give freely with all my heart.

Every day brings new opportunity and I happily start my day with enthusiasm.

I love, and I am proud, to be a woman. I am sensual, nurturing, compassionate and I am a goddess.

I am fearless, authentic and I am my ultimate truth. Everything I want is available to me.

I am the author of my life. I write the exciting, powerful, wonderful, and miraculous script of my life.

I acknowledge and appreciate the people who love and enriches my life.

I explore my abilities and bring them into a full manifestation. I am successful in everything I do.

I quiet my mind, enjoying the sounds of tranquillity; I shine brightly inside.

I allow my imagination to run free and open myself up to new discoveries and ideas.

I acknowledge and honour what I have achieved. I bathe in the relaxation and knowledge that everything is happening according to Divine plan.

I take excellent care of my body. I am strong and healthy, and I send love and healing to my physical self.

I have faith and I trust my decisions-making abilities. I follow my divine guidance.

I let my guard down and allow people to get to know me well. All my relationships are harmonious and loving.

I love spending time in nature connecting with the elementals and welcoming them to cleanse my energy and lift my spirit.

When my heart is filled with happiness, everyone around me benefits from the magic of happiness.

I love being colourful and allowing my authentic self to radiate and shine brightly.

Wonderful opportunities always present themselves to me. I create fun in my life with everything I do.

I love and accept each member of my family. We are all healed and loved unconditionally.

I accept all my past experiences and I move forward positively with new, exciting experiences.

I forgive myself completely, I am free, and I move forward positively. Whenever I am scared, I remember to focus on love.

It doesn't matter whether my parent love me. What matters most is that I love myself unconditionally.

I am grounded and centred. I choose wisdom and love in all my dealings with myself and others.

The more I focus on love, the more I attract miracles in my life. I am always flowing with the universe.

I love living in my peaceful, comfortable and tranquil home. My home is a peaceful sanctuary.

I reassure my inner child that I love it unconditionally every day. My love for myself is constant.

My consciousness is filled with colourful and positive thoughts. My brilliant mind loves learning something new every day.

I communicate clearly with my Angels and Guides. I truly express myself and I listen deeply and pay attention to their guidance.

I open my heart and mind fully to myself, so I can truly understand my deep and authentic feelings.

I have compassion and love for myself and I hold kind, accepting thoughts toward myself.

When I feel vulnerable or I make a mistake, I shift my energy by forgiving and loving myself deeply. I am love.

I am patient with myself, I give myself time to reflect and heal. I act respectfully towards myself.

I am truly grateful, and I give thanks and acknowledgment for every little thing I have in my life.

I speak kindly and lovingly toward myself and I move freely without any fear of being attacked by my ego or shamed by guilt.

I call back all my lost soul fragments that are bound in the past by hurtful experiences or psychic wounding. We are united; I am whole and complete again.

I stop punishing myself for my mistakes. I value my mistakes, because my mistakes help me to make the right decisions and choose wisely.

When I love myself, it becomes easier to love other people. When I don't hurt myself, I don't hurt others. The more I love myself, the more others will love me.

I don't allow society, parents, and friends' negative opinions to make me feel unworthy. The truth is, I am love, I am lovable, I accept this, and I know this is true.

I stop being afraid to open my heart to love. The more I open my heart to love, the more I receive love from myself and from others.

Nothing is ever lost in the Divine Mind. I trust the intelligence within me to show me the way and bring me everything that I need.

I erase all negative thought patterns from my consciousness and I declare for myself prosperity in all areas of my life.

My mind is very powerful and it creates everything that I desire, good or bad. Therefore, I choose wisely and manifest only what is best for me and my world.

Whatever happens to me, pleasant or unpleasant, it is a lesson presented to me to re-evaluate my decisions.

I am a Divine Being so I can create and reshape my life whenever I wish.

I enjoy working toward my goals and I am successful in everything I focus on.

I live in a plentiful universe. I accept good graciously and I say yes to receiving abundance.

I accept compliments graciously. It is alright to be praised and I allow myself to receive love.

I release all judgements of myself. I am doing the best I can, and I am perfect just the way I am.

I am worthy of tremendous love and I give and receive love with an open heart.

I value and appreciate myself deeply. I deserve the very best and I have an incredible, fulfilled life.

I am loving, honourable, and compassionate. I treat others as I would want to be treated.

My sexuality is healthy, and I accept my sexuality; it feels good.

I am magnificent. I do everything right and I love and cherish myself immensely.

I follow my Divine guidance and bring the ideas I receive into full manifestation.

Wonderful opportunities always present themselves to me. I have many options to choose from.

I am a shining light in this world and I happily share this light with everyone I meet.

I release all my worries and confusion to heaven. I know that heaven is helping and guiding me every day throughout my life.

My body, mind and spirit are in harmony and they vibrate love. I am constantly flowing with the universe.

I listen to the messages my body is conveying to me and I joyfully comply to my body's guidance.

I absolutely trust the intelligence within me to guide me always in my life's journey.

When I love and give love, I am contributing to this wonderful world.

Every day, I am learning, growing and expanding my consciousness. I am creating positiveness and contributing to the world.

Whenever I catch my ego chattering, I send it love and focus on all the wonderful things in my life.

I am connected to all of life. I live in a society where I am safe and free to express my uniqueness.

I understand that when one door closes, a better door opens. I am continuously growing and expanding.

I listen to beautiful music that resonates with me. I connect and dance beautifully.

I realise uncertainty and fear. I am eternally safe and amazing endless possibilities lies before me.

The universe is constantly delivering incredible gifts to me and I gratefully accept.

I am strong and confident enough to refuse something if it is not in my best interest.

I release all my worries to heaven and sleep peacefully. I awake feeling fresh and rejuvenated.

I love and accept my uniqueness because I am one-of-a-kind.

I attract remarkable experiences every day and I am loved and blessed by everyone.

I am working in a career that is fulfilling and rewarding.

I have a perfect tranquillity work in space and I am successful in every area of my life.

I congratulate myself for everything I have done. I deserve praise, even if I haven't accomplished a lot. It's important to acknowledge how far I have come. I thank myself for never giving up and continuing to climb higher mountains.

I cherish all my past experiences and I move forward positively with all my endeavours.

I am special and worthy of love. I am safe and perfect. I am free to do whatever makes me happy. I am a loving, happy person and everyone loves me. I bring joy wherever I go.

I am totally adequate at all times. I expect success in every area of my life and I recognise and accept every person I meet as an ally in my soul plan. I am receptive to all the abundance the universe has in store for me.

Whenever I feel overwhelmed and stressed, I meditate and imagine myself in a place that makes me happy.

THREE

Self-Gratitude Affirmations Directed to God

Gratitude to God and our Guides

Thank you, God, for your unconditional love and protection. Thank you for my beautiful life and my perfect health.

Thank you for my brilliant mind that knows no limits. Thank you for my abundance in life and the never-ending supplies. Thank you for helping and guiding me with everything in my life.

I love you, God.

Thank you, thank you, thank you, God.

Thank you, my Higher-Self, for your unconditional love and protection.

Thank you for removing all blocks and interference in my life.

Thank you for helping me and guiding me with everything in my life.

I love you, my Higher-Self.

Thank you, thank you, thank you, my Higher-Self.

Thank you, my Guardian Angels, for your unconditional love and protection. Thank you for helping and guiding me with everything in my life.

I love you, my Guardian Angels. Thank you, thank you, thank you, Guardian Angels.

Thank you, my Spirit Guides, for your unconditional love and protection. Thank you for helping and guiding me, with everything in my lifetime.

I love you, my Spirit Guides. Thank you, thank you, thank you, Spirit Guides.

Thank you, Archangels, for your unconditional love and protection. Thank you for helping and guiding me with everything in my life.

I love you, Archangels. Thank you, thank you, thank you, Archangels.

Thank you, Jesus, for your unconditional love and protection. Thank you for helping and guiding me with everything in life.

I love you, Jesus.

Thank you, thank you, thank you, Jesus.

Thank you, Mother Mary, for your unconditional love and protection. Thank you for guiding and helping me with everything in my life.

I love you, Mother Mary.

Thank you, thank you, thank you, Mother Mary.

Thank you, Mary Magdalene, for your unconditional love and protection. Thank you for guiding and helping me with everything in my life.

I love you, Mary Magdalene.

Thank you, thank you, thank you, Mary Magdalene.

I am truly grateful for my life. Thank you, God, for my wonderful life. I love my life and life loves me.
Thank You, Thank You, Thank You, God.

I am truly grateful for my health. Thank You, God, for my perfect health. I am healthy, and I love my body.
Thank You, Thank You, Thank You, God.

I am truly grateful for all the love I have in my life. I am surrounded

by love, and I love myself unconditionally.
Thank You, Thank You, Thank You, God.

I am truly grateful for my happiness. I am happy, and I have a comfortable home. I am surrounded by happy and loving people.
Thank You, Thank You, Thank You, God.

I am truly grateful for my relationships. I have an excellent relationship with myself. I have loving, supportive people in my life.
Thank You, Thank You, Thank You, God.

I am truly grateful for all my passions. I am passionate about my life, career, creativity, and everything I am learning. I have a brilliant mind.
Thank You, Thank You, Thank You, God.

I am truly grateful for who I am. I love myself, unconditionally. I am happy, loving, caring, healthy, focused, confident, creative, and responsible. I am passionate about my divinity and everything I do. I have a brilliant mind that knows no limit.
Thank You, Thank You, Thank You, God.

I am truly grateful for my beautiful body. I have a healthy, strong, and flexible body. I love my body, the way I look and everything about my body. I honour and respect my body.
Thank You, Thank You, Thank You, God.

I am truly grateful for the sound of my voice. I love my voice, and I speak beautifully with confidence.
Thank You, Thank You, Thank You, God.

I am truly grateful for my strong, healthy heart. My heart is open

and capable of tremendous love. I love my heart.
Thank You, Thank You, Thank You, God.

I am truly grateful for my ability to exercise. I am motivated to exercise, and exercise makes me feel good. I love nourishing and looking after my body.
Thank You, Thank You, Thank You, God.

I am truly grateful I can meditate. I love meditating and connecting within and receive the answers I seek.
Thank You, Thank You, Thank You, God.

I am truly grateful for all the money I am receiving every day and month. Thank You, God, for all the expected and unexpected money coming to me.
Thank You, Thank You, Thank You, God.

I am truly grateful for my work. I have a peaceful and spacious working space. I have great working colleagues, and we work as a team and in harmony
Thank You, Thank You, Thank You, God.

I am truly grateful for all my material needs being met. I am worthy and thankful for all the abundance in my life.
Thank You, Thank You, Thank You, God.

I am truly grateful for home. My home is a peaceful haven. I love my tranquil home.
Thank You, Thank You, Thank You, God.

I am truly grateful for my car. I love my beautiful car that takes me everywhere and provides comfort.

Thank You, Thank You, Thank You, God.

I am truly grateful for my everyday life. I spend every day with ease and happiness, and every day is a beautiful adventure.
Thank You, Thank You, Thank You, God.

I am truly grateful and happy that I can afford to have wonderful holidays with my family and friends.
Thank You, Thank You, Thank You, God.

Family Gratitude Affirmations

I am truly grateful for my family. I love my family, and my family loves me. I have a loving, happy, and supportive family.
Thank You, Thank You, Thank You, God.

I am truly grateful for my son /name/ Thank You, God, for my sons' /name/ life.
My son is healthy, happy, loving, caring, confident, responsible, and focused. My son goes to a great school that he loves. My son has loving,

attentive teachers and great friends who are a good influence on him. My son has a brilliant creative mind.
Thank You, Thank You, Thank You, God.

I am truly grateful for my daughter/name/
Thank You, God, for my daughter's /name/ life. My daughter is healthy, happy, loving, caring, confident, responsible, and focused. My daughter goes to a great school that she loves. My daughter has loving, attentive teachers and great friends who are good influence on her. My daughter has a brilliant creative mind.
Thank You, Thank You, Thank You, God.

I am truly grateful for my children. Thank You, God, for my children's lives. My children are healthy, caring, loving, happy, confident, responsible, and focused. My children go to a great school that they love. My children have loving and attentive teachers and great friends who have a good influence on them. My children have brilliant creative minds.
Thank You, Thank You, Thank You, God.

I am truly grateful for my partner /name/ I have a wonderful loving and supportive partner. My partner loves and respects me. I am in a beautiful relationship with my soulmate.

Thank You, Thank You, Thank You, God.

I am truly grateful for my mother. I have a wonderful and loving relationship with my mother. We cherish and love each other. My mother is very supportive of me.
Thank You, Thank You, Thank You, God.

I am truly grateful for my father. I have a wonderful and loving relationship with my father. We cherish and love each other. My father is very supportive of me.
Thank You, Thank You, Thank You, God.

I am truly grateful for all my siblings. I have a close and loving relationship with my siblings. We cherish and support each other with everything we do.
Thank You, Thank You, Thank You, God.

I am truly grateful for my friends. I love and appreciate my friends. I have loving and supportive friends, and we have so much fun together.
Thank You, Thank You, Thank You, God.

Mother Earth Gratitude Affirmations

I am truly grateful for our beautiful Planet. I love all the exquisite wonders in our world. I love our Mother Earth.
Thank You, Thank You, Thank You, God.

I am truly grateful for the air I breathe. I love breathing in the fresh air, which rejuvenates my vitality.
Thank You, Thank You, Thank You, God.

I am truly grateful for the Elementals. Thank You Elementals for looking after my plants, flowers, gardens and for working with me. I welcome your help and guidance.
Thank You, Thank You, Thank You, God.

I am truly grateful for the Moon. I love gazing at the beautiful Moon, which fills me with happiness and a sense of purpose.
Thank You, Thank You, Thank You, God.

I am truly grateful for our Sun. I love feeling the sun on my skin, which rejuvenates and vitalise my body. The Sun makes me feel happy and healthy.
Thank You, Thank You, Thank You, God.

I am truly grateful for the trees. I love listening to the trees and feeling their gentle breeze on my skin. I love listening to the trees and connecting with them.
Thank You, Thank You, Thank You, God.

I am truly grateful for our beautiful parks. I love walking through the park, connecting with nature and observing the scenery. I enjoy walking bare feet on the grass, which makes me centred and grounded.
Thank You, Thank You, Thank You, God.

I am truly grateful for our amazing beautiful animals. I am thankful for the love and happiness they bring into my life.
Thank You, Thank You, Thank You, God.

I am truly grateful for our non-domestic animals. I love seeing these truly magnificent animals.
Thank You, Thank You, Thank You, God.

I am truly grateful for our beautiful breathtaking ocean. I love swimming in the sea, the sea cleanses my body and mind and rejuvenates me.
Thank You, Thank You, Thank You, God.

FOUR

How Affirmations Can Change Your Life

Re-programming your subconscious mind and knowing how to change your approach at any given moment.

"No matter what is going on in my life, I stay optimistic and positive."

We sometimes have days when things are going worse, and nothing seems to work.

It is easy to lay blame, criticise others, and beat ourselves up—which allows more negative energies to creep in and add to our vulnerability. We must find the strength and courage to shift our energy by focusing on one positive thing. Expand it from there, utilizing affirmations or meditation to shift our energy. It's part of the growth, so do your best to be positive.

"I am a Divine Being, and I am loved and cherished by my creator."

Worthiness doesn't mean you have done something right or are perceived as being excellent—or worthy—by others. You are a Divine Being, so you are worthy no matter what. Don't block your manifestations due to deep-seated beliefs that you don't deserve good. You are loved unconditionally and cherished by your Creator.

"I am doing what I am meant to do, and I am prosperous."

Sometimes, we find it challenging to decide on what we really want. Or if we do know what we want, we are scared of the unknown and worried whether our life purpose would bring us happiness and fulfilment. Especially if we already have a job that provides for our material needs but not fulfilling spiritually.

If we are not doing what we are meant to be doing, we get tired, stressed, frustrated and empty. We must have blind faith and trust the intelligence within us, knowing that we can only have absolute abundance in all areas of our lives if we are doing what we are here to do. Consequently, help others in their journey.

"I am capable, and my dominant thoughts are positive."

Focus on your strength instead of your weakness. Focus your energy on what you want and make your dominant thoughts positive.

"I am perfect and loved by my creator."

Remembering to pray when we feel down and low. Prayers lift us to that state of being whole and loved.

"I forgive easily, and I am full of love."

Love heals everything, and forgiveness and love is the way forward. Don't allow anyone to cause you to close your heart.

"I connect within and receive all the answers I seek."

We are always searching for answers out there; however, the answers we seek are within us. We just need to quiet our mind and look within.

"I quiet my mind and connect with my guides."

Our guides are always with us, guiding and protecting us. We can ask for their help at any time. We connect with these Heavenly Beings by quieting our mind and meditating.

"I ease my mind and focus on what I want."

Anything we force to happen adds stress and negative energy to it. Whether working on a project or doing what you love, do it with ease, fun and love. Then the negative blocks are removed, and you manifest what you want quickly.

"I stand my ground and follow my heart."

You must stand your ground and believe in yourself. Don't let others intimidate you into giving up.

"I am magnificent; I am loved unconditionally by my Creator."

We are balanced and healed when we connect within. We are loved unconditionally by our Creator.

"I trust in Divine Timing, and I focus on gratitude."

When life becomes difficult, remember the power of gratitude. Perhaps you have been feeling sorry for yourself lately or feeling as if God has forgotten about you. Have faith that your prayers are answered in many different ways. Allow yourself to notice all of the gifts and blessings you already have and focus on gratitude.

"I am healed inside out, and I am in perfect health."

Laugh a certain number of times per day as your Divine

Prescription. If you are going through recovery of any kind, laughter will speed up your recovery. Also, alternative medicine like energy healing will heal and balance your energy from the inside, which is where the healing must start before a full recovery is received.

"I open my heart and let God and the Angels help me."

My brothers and sisters let's make our journey here on Earth magnificent. You can start today to make a difference in your life and the people around you. If you feel stuck, let God and the Angels into your heart.

"I am optimistic, and my mind is clear."

Living in a 3-D world can be challenging. However, let's focus our predominant thoughts on the positive things in our lives.

"I love Meditating and receiving the answers I need."

Meditating, even for five minutes a day, can help manage stress and lead to a healthy lifestyle. Meditation is a beautiful way to connect with your Higher Self, Guardian Angels and Spirit Guides and receive the answers you seek.

"I connect with my loved ones in heaven and receive the healing and guidance I need."

Losing a loved one can be heartbreaking. However, no one dies in truth; our souls are eternal.

You can talk to your loved ones and ask them for signs—they can hear you. You can also connect with them through dream visitation. If you are finding it difficult to move on, or to understand why things happened the way they did and need answers, you can consult a Medium and receive the answers you seek to help you. Your loved ones are always watching, guiding, and protecting you.

"I am powerfully capable, and I love my uniqueness."

Express your uniqueness and believe you are perfect every way. If you can't, or someone or something is stopping you, look within and start healing yourself from the inside out. Don't allow anyone to dull your spark.

"I release all of my stress. I am centred, grounded, and I am healed."

Stress can have a detrimental impact on your body which leads to unpleasant issues in your body. No matter what's going on in your life, focus on perfect health. Meditate to connect within.

"I love my inner child deeply."

Have you said, "I love you" to yourself today? Let your inner child know how much you love it. Loving yourself is fundamental.

"Water purifies my cells and I love swimming in the ocean."

Spend time near water, river, the ocean, or soak in a sea salt bath or freshwater to recharge your battery. Water's curative effects are well known and documented.

Water can wash away sadness, pain, and the ill effects of suffering. Water is very healing because the human body is composed almost entirely of water.

"I eat healthfully, and I am vibrant."

Maintaining our energy level is vital to health and healing. Eating a high energy diet and avoiding eating energy draining food and beverages can help with our well-being.

"I listen to my body's messages and comply happily."

Trust your intuition, dreams, feelings, and body. God and the Angels speak to you every day; however, you need to quiet your mind to hear their guidance.

Also, your body is brilliant; it gives you a warning before you manifest anything unpleasant. So, trust your feelings and your knowingness to guide you to a happy, healthier you.

"I choose wisely, and I believe in myself."

Believe in yourself and see yourself doing the things you love. Every day is a new day to choose wisely and change your circumstances. Focus on what you want and what you don't will disappear.

"I trust my Guides and Angels, and I listen to their guidance."

Our Guardian Angels and Guides are always with us and guiding and helping us. They send us signs every day so pay attention.

You can also get a reading and find out what these Benevolent Beings have to tell you. Involve them in your daily life and watch the magic happen.

"I make time and connect with my inner child."

Balance is everything, don't stress yourself. Make time to play and connect with your inner child.

"I am always paying attention to the signs around me."

Pay attention and notice the signs around you. Heaven is always sending you signs to help you. You may see feathers, smell a scent, or find coins. Don't dismiss the signs you receive and don't mistake synchronistic events for mere coincidence.

"I give and receive equally with an open heart."

If you just give, you block the flow, and if you only receive, you block the flow. Balance the flow of giving and receiving.

Whatever you want to manifest, ask Heaven to help you and know that your prayers are answered. Open your arms with gratitude and be grateful for everything you have to open the gates of manifestation.

We tend to reward others and forget about ourselves. Reword yourself and balance giving and receiving to keep the energy flowing.

"I connect and reassure my inner child, how much I love it."

Healing starts within, check in with your inner child to make sure she/he is happy. Your inner child happiness is fundamental. Connect often with your inner child and reassure it of your love.

"I approach all my situations with positivity and love."

Focus on the positive in life. Don't get pulled into anyone's drama; it lowers your energy. Whenever you find yourself in an uncomfortable situation, focus on love and send healing. The positive approach brings a positive solution.

"I give and receive with joy and gratitude."

This is an abundant universe filled with more than enough for everyone. Balance is the key, so fearlessly give and receive with joy and gratitude. It's like breathing; both inhale and exhale are equally important.

"I Bless my water before drinking it to increase my energy and vitality."

Water is the best incomparable beverage for our body. Symptoms such as fatigue, difficulty in concentrating, irritation and excessive hunger can actually be dehydration. It's a good idea to bless the water before drinking it.

"By doing what I love, I am setting a good example."

Say, "Yes" to life, follow your heart to desire and manifest your dreams. Life can be magnificent if you want it that way. Remember, when you prosper, you are helping others to follow suit.

"I am surrounded and supported by divine love."

Love keeps us connected to our Creator and the Angels. The more we love, the more we are connected to God. Don't allow anyone to give you a reason to dim your light, no matter what challenges you are facing, keep the love going.

God is love; God is everywhere and within everyone. Therefore, Divine Love is surrounding, healing, and supporting you.

"I love learning new skills and nurturing my mind."

In many ways, we are like a blossoming flower and ready to open and grow. Let's enjoy learning new knowledge and skills. Take our time to accumulate new ideas and nurture our mind.

"I love dancing with the universe and celebrating my life's remarkable journey."

The old must be released so that the new can enter. The dance of the universe is a happy one with energy swirling in a never-ending celebration of life itself. Join this dance, and don't fear change. Your strength and growth can come from your deepest emotions, which can be healing educational and also rewarding. Embrace it as evidence that you are a life.

"I clear and shield my energy every morning and evening."

For we who are sensitive, we need to shield ourselves and protect our energy. We can imagine white light and pink light surrounding us. Or simply request the Angels to cover us with Angelic light and just know that we are spiritually and emotionally protected.

Sometimes our moods change frequently, and we don't understand why. It because we are affected by the people and energies around us. Shield yourself every morning and ask the Angels to clear your energy in the evening before bed.

"I am gentle and loving towards myself."

It's imperative to show gentleness toward our self. We may see aspects within us that cause us to worry or become impatient. But every person is a child of God. We must balance all aspects of ourselves with love and mercy before we can exhibit those same qualities to the people around us.

We are stronger than we may believe. Every situation we find ourselves in requires a soft and sensitive approach. Archangel Ariel can help us stay strong in every challenging situation.

"I am always changing and growing positively."

We are changing the energies around us frequently. We shouldn't be afraid of change; it's part of our growth. Joy reminds us that we don't need to suffer.

We can accomplish our purpose, help ourselves and others and heal through the power of pleasure. Let's stay positive and focus on what brings us joy.

"I respect and speak kindly about my body."

Every part of our body has a voice, so listen and follow its guidance.

However, if we ignore our bodies messages, it will speak intensively louder in the form of pain etc.

Let's honour our beautiful vessel, treating and feeding it well and talking about our body positively. Affirm daily to your body: "I love you; I am grateful for the way I feel, the way I look, and I am in perfect health."

"I ask for Divine assistance whenever I need it."

You have Divine counsellors around you, so tell them your worries, feelings, and what you need help with. Your Guardian Angels and Spirit Guides are ready to help you. All you have to do is ask them and have faith.

"I am working toward enlightenment."

As a species, the only way we can survive is by working together in authenticity, generosity, love, and appreciation and knowing that we are brothers and sisters on a journey to enlightenment.

"I am love, and I spread love wherever I go."

Let's remember that the only thing we take with us to heaven is the love that we have shared.

Let's open our hearts as big as we can muster and share the love that we are capable of with every person we come into contact with, no matter how small.

"I enthusiastically live every day to the fullest."

Let's spend every day enthusiastically, with great appreciation for life, and strive to be more and better than yesterday.

"I work in harmony with everyone I meet"

As eternal divine beings, when we are coming from love, and our intentions are for the whole, everything is made available to us. We can only help each other and our evolution if we are coming from the heart and working as a collective.

Printed in Great Britain
by Amazon

86303886R00098